YORKIES

FAVORITE DOG BREEDS

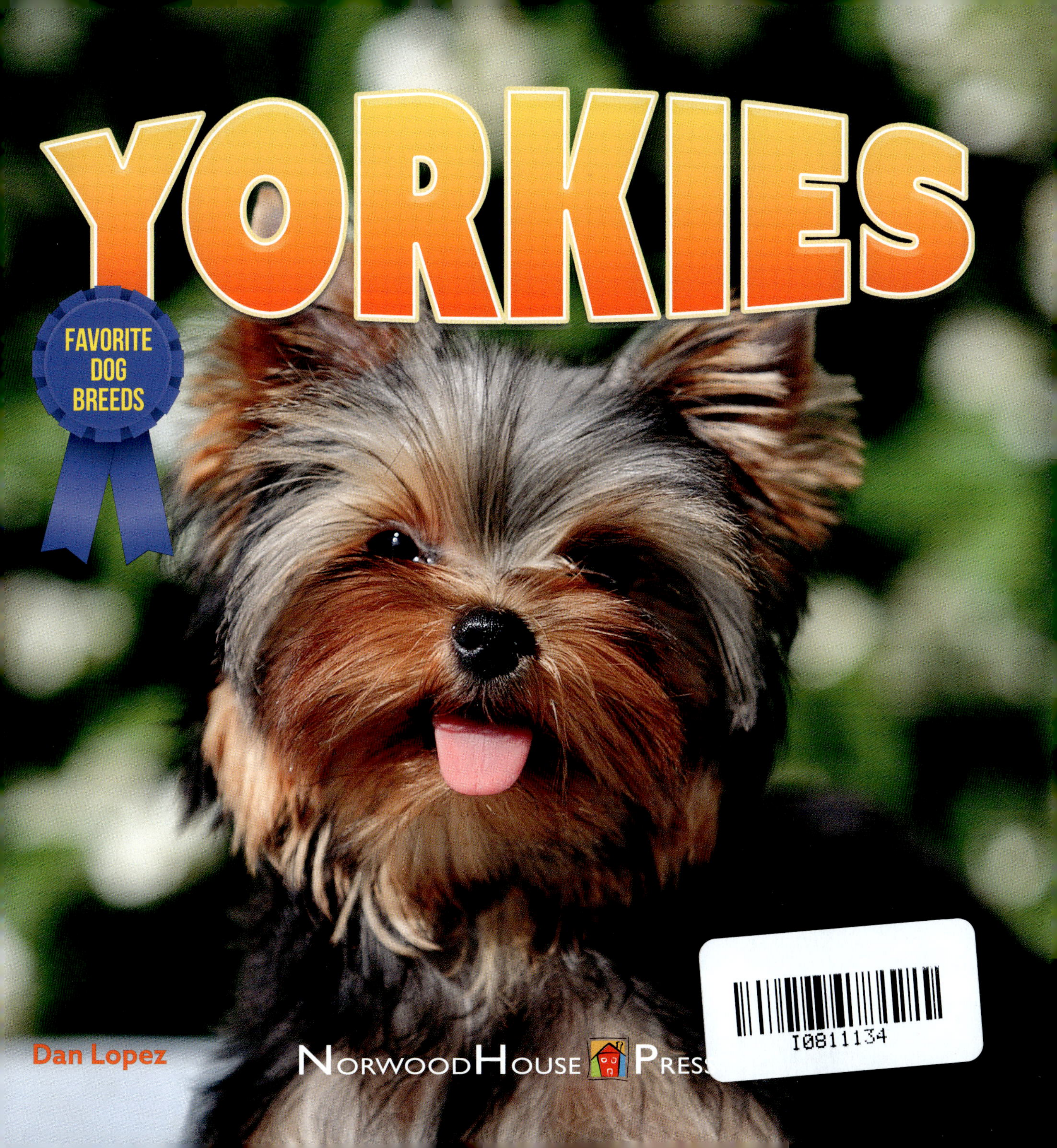

Dan Lopez

NorwoodHouse Press

Cataloging-in-Publication Data

Names: Lopez, Dan.
Title: Yorkies / Dan Lopez.
Description: Buffalo, NY : Norwood House Press, 2026. | Series: Favorite dog breeds| Includes glossary and index.
Identifiers: ISBN 9781978576711 (pbk.) | ISBN 9781978576728 (library bound) | ISBN 9781978576735 (ebook)
Subjects: LCSH: Yorkshire terrier--Juvenile literature.
Classification: LCC SF429.Y6 L67 2026 | DDC 636.76--dc23

Published in 2026 by
Norwood House Press
2544 Clinton Street
Buffalo, NY 14224

Designer: Rhea Magaro
Editor: Kim Thompson

Photo credits: Cover, p. 1 Margarita Zhuravleva, Giraphics /Shutterstock.com; pp. 4, 12, 13 Wikipedia; p. 5 Vojce/Shutterstock.com; p. 6 Steve Bruckmann/Shutterstock.com; p. 8 Phase4Studios/Shutterstock.com; p. 9 AndrWater/Shutterstock.com; p. 10 Eve Photography/Shutterstock.com; p. 14 Rawpixel.com/Shuttersock.com; p. 17 Przemek Iciak/ Shutterstock.com; p. 18 Oksana Shufrych/Shutterstock.com; p. 19 Annette Shaff/Shutterstock.com; p. 20 Serdar Tibet/Shutterstock.com; p. 21 Anna Averianova/Shutterstock.com

Printed in the United States of America

CPSIA compliance information: Batch #CWNHP26: For further information contact Norwood House Press at 1-800-237-9932.

TABLE OF CONTENTS

Meet the Yorkshire Terrier

Yorkshire terriers are popular pets. They are often called Yorkies. This **breed** is known for its tiny size and long, flowing hair.

Toto, the dog from *The Wizard of Oz*, is a Yorkie.

What Do Yorkies Look Like?

Yorkies belong to a category of tiny dogs called toy dogs. A Yorkie can grow to about nine inches (23 centimeters) tall. It can weigh up to seven pounds (three kilograms).

A Yorkie has pointed ears that stand up straight. It has dark, round, shining eyes.

Many owners choose to **dock** their Yorkies' tails.

Yorkies have fine, silky fur that can flow all the way to the ground. It comes in shades of silver-blue, black, and tan.

Many owners trim their Yorkies' hair. They fasten bows to their heads.

Where Do Yorkies Come From?

Yorkies were first raised in Yorkshire, England, in the 1800s. Some of their owners were weavers who worked in **mills**. Their little Yorkies helped them by darting under machinery to catch rats.

The weavers joked that they used their **looms** to make the Yorkies' beautiful, long hair.

People admired the workers' Yorkies. They wanted them as pets. It became popular for rich **Victorian** ladies to keep Yorkies and other small dogs as **lapdogs**.

Do Yorkies Make Good Pets?

Little Yorkies have big personalities. They are **feisty** and full of energy.

When they want their own way, Yorkies can be bossy. Even so, they are fun pets who often make their owners laugh.

Yorkies are **hypoallergenic**, so they are good for people with allergies.

Yorkies are brave and **loyal**. They are not afraid to bark at strangers. They make good **watchdogs**.

What Do Yorkies Need?

A Yorkie's hair needs special care. These dogs need weekly baths and daily brushing.

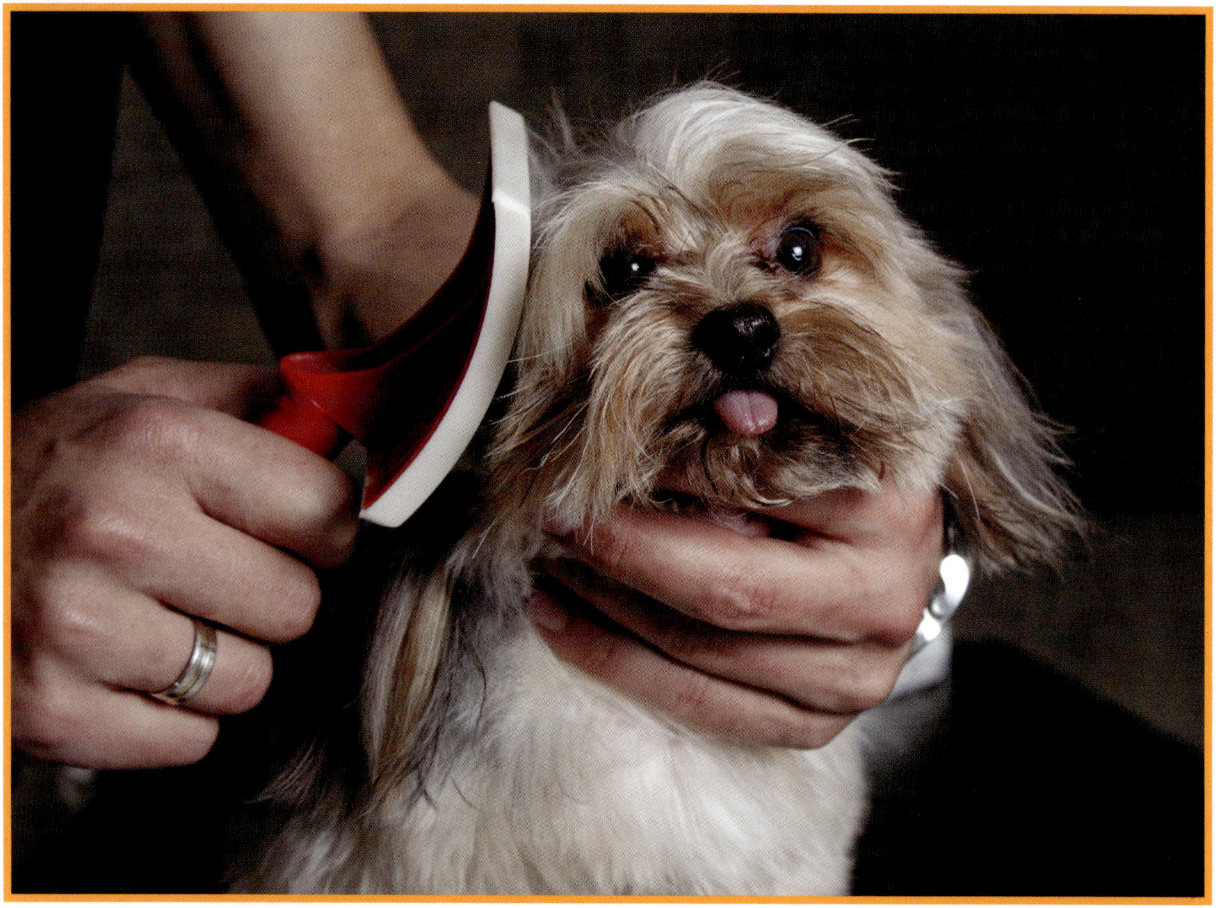

Exercise is also important. Yorkies enjoy short, active games such as chasing balls.

Glossary

breed (breed): one type or kind of an animal

dock (dahk): to cut short

feisty (FYE-stee): lively, frisky, and spirited

hypoallergenic (hye-poh-a-luhr-JE-nik): unlikely to cause an allergic reaction

lapdogs (LAP-dawgs): small dogs that may be held in the lap

looms (loomz): machines used for weaving yarn or threads into cloth

loyal (LOI-uhl): faithful and true to someone or something

mills (milz): factories that produce cloth

Victorian (vik-TOR-ee-uhn): related to the rule of Queen Victoria in England in the mid- to late-1800s; a time when people wore corsets, bonnets, top hats, bustles, and petticoats

watchdogs (WAHCH-dawgs): dogs kept to guard property

Thinking Questions

1. Describe a Yorkie's fur.
2. What is a toy dog?
3. Where do Yorkies get their name?
4. Describe a Yorkie's personality.
5. What special care do Yorkies need?

Index

About the Author

Dan Lopez is a writer who loves dogs! He has a German shepherd named Hans and an Irish setter named Tam. They love to go for walks in the woods together. Sometimes, they jump in the lake for a swim. Dan lives in Indiana with his wife and three kids.